REPRINTS OF ECONOMIC CLASSICS

LAPSES FROM FULL EMPLOYMENT

LAPSES FROM FULL EMPLOYMENT

BY

A. C. PIGOU, M.A.

SOMETIME PROFESSOR OF POLITICAL ECONOMY
IN THE UNIVERSITY OF CAMBRIDGE

AUGUSTUS M. KELLEY · PUBLISHERS
FAIRFIELD 1978

First edition 1945
(London: Macmillan & Co., Ltd., 1945)

Reprinted 1978 by

AUGUSTUS M. KELLEY · PUBLISHERS
Fairfield, New Jersey 07006
By arrangement with Macmillan & Co. Ltd.

Library of Congress Cataloging in Publication Data

Pigou, Arthur Cecil, 1877-1959.
  Lapses from full employment.

  (Reprints of economic classics)
  Reprint of the 1945 ed. published by Macmillan, London.
  1. Unemployed. 2. Full employment policies.
I. Title.
HD5706.P46   1977   331.1'37   76-52488
ISBN 0-678-01226-1

MANUFACTURED IN THE UNITED STATES OF AMERICA

PREFACE

THE purpose of this short book is to provide a background for the discussion of practical schemes for attacking the problem of unemployment. It does not itself discuss any of these schemes, but seeks to disentangle from one another and to set out in clear light some of the principal influences by which the employment situation is affected. The analysis is conducted from the money end, not, as in my *Theory of Unemployment*, from the real end. I have tried to make it simple and intelligible, at the cost of a little trouble, to readers not trained in economics.[1] But I have an uneasy feeling that, whether through my own deficiencies or because of the nature of the subject, I have not succeeded in this. Some parts of the argument unpractised readers — maybe others also — will almost certainly find difficult. I am sorry about this, but cannot help it. At least they have been warned. Professor Dennis Robertson, who has very kindly read my proofs, has warned me that the form of the book may suggest that I am in favour of attacking the problem of unemployment by manipulating wages rather than by manipulating demand. I wish, therefore, to say clearly that this is not so. In the present state of fact and opinion I am broadly in sympathy with the lines of approach suggested in the White Paper on Unemployment Policy. But the subject matter of this book is not policy at all, only diagnosis.

[1] A more thorough treatment is attempted in my books on *Industrial Fluctuations*, *The Theory of Unemployment* and *Employment and Equilibrium*.

A. C. P.

KING'S COLLEGE, CAMBRIDGE
November 1944

CONTENTS

Chapter		Page
I.	INTRODUCTION	1
II.	A FORMAL ANALYSIS	6
III.	WAGE RATES AND UNEMPLOYMENT	10
IV.	THOROUGH-GOING COMPETITION AMONG WAGE-EARNERS	18
V.	THE CLASSICAL VIEW	20
VI.	THE ACTUAL LEVEL OF WAGE RATES	26
VII.	THE DISTRIBUTION OF WAGE RATES AND UNEMPLOYMENT	30
VIII.	THE DEMAND FOR LABOUR AND UNEMPLOYMENT	38
IX.	FLUCTUATIONS IN THE AGGREGATE DEMAND FOR LABOUR AND UNEMPLOYMENT	40
X.	THE DISTRIBUTION OF FLUCTUATIONS OF DEMAND FOR LABOUR AMONG DIFFERENT CENTRES	52
XI.	MOVEMENTS OF LABOUR IN RELATION TO UNEMPLOYMENT	57
XII.	STABILISING THE DEMAND FOR LABOUR	69

CHAPTER I

INTRODUCTION

Two goals of policy in the field of employment have been widely proclaimed. The one is the abolition of mass unemployment, the other the establishment and maintenance of full employment. The former phrase, for which Sir William Beveridge is responsible, means, as I understand it, doing away with that hard core of unemployment, particularly perhaps the unemployment lasting, for a number of men, over many months or several years, which persisted in the coal-mining industry and in the depressed areas during most of the period between the two wars. Naturally everybody would like to abolish mass unemployment in that sense. The phrase, if not particularly illuminating — for mass unemployment is not a particular kind of unemployment that can be separated off from other kinds — is at least harmless. That cannot be said of the slogan about full employment. Anybody taking words in their natural sense would suppose that, when employment is full, not of course everybody in existence, but everybody who at the ruling rates of wage wishes to be employed, is in fact employed. But certain economists, and, following them, many journalists have come to use the term full employment in a special technical sense to signify that there is no unemployment due to investment being too small, or no cyclical unemployment or, it may be, no unemployment of some other special sort. Thus for them full employment may prevail in spite of the fact that a large number of persons are unemployed, because, for example, they are moving about from one job to another or have failed to move away from depressed areas or occupations where their services are no longer wanted. When these persons speak about maintaining full employment after the war they are using the term in a special technical sense; but the ordinary reader may easily think that they are using it in the literal sense. Since it is frequently argued that full employment in one or another special sense *could* be established and maintained in this country if certain remedies for unemployment were adopted, it has come to be widely believed that full employment in the literal sense could be established and maintained. No economist believes that. Even to-day in the high tide of war activity full employment in the literal sense does not exist. Anybody who imagines that it can be made to exist after the war is living in a fool's paradise. That professional writers should have appropriated a term with a perfectly obvious common-sense meaning and used it with a quite different meaning, thus causing confusion in the public mind, is much to be regretted. For my own part in this book I shall use the term full employment always and only to mean what it literally says — that and nothing else. So using it, I do not regard the establishment and maintenance of full employment after the war as a practicable objective. The concept is serviceable only as a statistical norm, with which states of employment that have existed, do exist, or might be made to exist can be compared.

The difference between full employment in the literal sense and actual employment in any period is unemployment. It is this difference that is interesting and important. I have put the phrase full employment into my title so as to conform with the fashion; but, as the other words in that title make plain, it is lapses from full employment — in the literal, not the technical, sense — that is to say unemployment, that the book is really about.

Employment and unemployment are elliptical expressions. Employment and unemployment of what? By convention we mean employment and unemployment of

INTRODUCTION

weekly wage-earners, of whom the great bulk are now insured against unemployment under the Unemployment Insurance Act and about whose condition elaborate statistics are published at regular intervals in the *Labour Gazette*. It should be borne in mind, however, that these weekly wage-earners — labour, as we are accustomed to say — are not the whole, but only a part, of the productive resources of the country, and, what is important here, that other productive resources, salary-earners and material instruments of production, are also liable to be employed or unemployed in varying degrees. When a number of wage-earners are out of work a number of machines, which they might have operated, are likely to be idle, ships which they might have sailed laid up, blast furnaces blown out. It would be wrong to think, as the phrasing of some economic textbooks might perhaps suggest, that quantities of labour, varying from time to time, are "applied" to a stock of capital, the whole of which is in use continuously. In general, employment for labour and employment for capital vary in the same sense, more (or less) employment for the one being accompanied by more (or less) employment for the other also. This fact obviously makes the relation between variations in the employment of labour and variations in the output of industry different from what it would otherwise have been, and is, from that point of view, important. Here, however, it is the employment and unemployment of *labour* that we are concerned to discuss.

What is the relation between employment and unemployment? *Given the number of persons seeking work*, it is obvious that 10 per cent unemployment implies 90 per cent employment; and that a rise from 10 to 20 per cent in unemployment implies a fall from 90 to 80 per cent in employment, *i.e.* a fall of approximately 11 per cent; and so on generally. But, if the number of persons seeking work is not given, though it is still true that 10 per cent unemployment at any time implies 90 per cent employment, the second relationship described above no longer holds good. For example, suppose that between two dates the number of persons seeking work anywhere increases from 100 to 150, *i.e.* by 50 per cent, and the percentage unemployed rises from 10 to 20 per cent of the original number seeking work. The number employed will not have fallen from 90 to 80 per cent, but risen from 90 to 130 per cent of this original number. The change by 10 per cent in the percentage of persons unemployed will not carry with it anything approaching an equivalent change in the percentage of persons employed. In particular occupations the numbers of persons seeking work are, of course, liable to vary largely, so that inferences about employment changes between different dates cannot be safely drawn from recorded percentages of unemployment at those dates. For the community as a whole this difficulty is less serious, because transfers of would-be wage-earners between different occupations are not relevant.

It must be remembered that even the aggregate number of would-be wage-earners is not fixed — would not, indeed, be fixed even though the size of the population of working age was stationary. For a person who is not employed because he does not wish to be employed is not ordinarily counted as belonging to the unemployed.[1] We may speak of the idle rich, if we will, but not of the unemployed rich. Unemployment is thus a condition of involuntary, not of voluntary idleness. The number of persons who

[1] With this definition a married woman who succeeds in drawing unemployment benefit by pretending that she is a would-be wage-earner when in fact she has decided to withdraw from industry is not unemployed. During the post-war slump of 1920–22 the regulations made it possible for a fair number of women who were not unemployed in my sense to do this, and so to be included in the official statistics of unemployment. In general, however, this kind of thing does not happen to any appreciable extent. For a fuller discussion of this compare my *Theory of Unemployment*, Part I, ch. i.

INTRODUCTION

wish to be employed is always liable to be affected in some degree by variations in wage rates. High wages, for example, may, on the one hand, attract to work men who might have retired; on the other hand, may dispense from work women whose husbands they have made better off. Here, however, that consideration, which is not quantitatively very important, will be ignored.

Even with this reservation no attempt is made in the discussion that follows to treat the problem of unemployment exhaustively. Throughout the complications connected with differences among work-people, whether due to inborn qualities or to training, are left on one side, and the argument is conducted as though all of them were similar. Attention is confined to three dominating influences: those, namely, that are associated with the relation between wage rates and demands for labour, disturbances in demands for labour, and movements of labour. Nor is any attempt made to formulate remedies for unemployment. The discussion is confined to diagnosis. Down to the end of Chapter VIII we shall be thinking in the main about conditions that are fairly stable and, thereafter, shall bring into account problems connected with industrial fluctuations

CHAPTER II

A FORMAL ANALYSIS

WE suppose that the number of persons seeking work is independent of the money rate of wages; that this rate is the same everywhere (for persons of similar quality); and that labour is perfectly mobile among all centres of employment, so that, in effect, there is a single money demand schedule for labour confronting all work-people. We further suppose *for the moment* that the rate of wages and this demand schedule are wholly independent of one another, so that the money rate of wages is the same whatever happens to the demand schedule and the demand schedule is the same whatever happens to the money rate of wages. Thus we have to do with three independent elements: the number of people seeking work, the money rate of wages, and the demand schedule for labour as a whole. The two former of these elements need no discussion, but it is desirable to make clear at the outset what precisely is meant by the third

I

The money demand schedule for labour as a whole describes a list of demand prices that are offered for hiring various quantities of labour — differences among types of labour being for our purpose ignored. It is derived from the money demand schedule for output (or real income) as a whole. That money demand schedule can only in given conditions have a single form, namely, a form such that quantity of output multiplied by price, that is money outlay or money income, is the same irrespective of what the quantity of output is. A curve drawn to represent a demand schedule of this type will,

A FORMAL ANALYSIS

of course, be a rectangular hyperbola.

The money demand schedule for labour as a whole derived from this money demand schedule for output as a whole has a mathematical relation to the parent demand schedule, the character of which depends on whether employers compete freely with one another for the favours of customers or exercise some degree of monopoly power.

In the former case the demand price for 1000 units of labour is equal to the price of a unit of product, when 1000 units of labour are at work, multiplied by the difference made to the total output by the presence of the 1000th unit of labour. If the representative employer is exercising monopoly power, the demand price per unit for 1000 units of labour is less than this, being smaller the less elastic is the demand for the output of the representative employer.

There is no necessity either under pure competition or under any given degree of monopoly for the demand schedule for labour as a whole to have the same form as that of the parent demand schedule. For it to have that form implies that the proportion of aggregate income which accrues to labour is the same irrespective of the quantity of labour that is being employed. There is some statistical evidence suggesting that for this country, as also for the United States, that implication fits the facts more nearly than we might be inclined to expect *a priori*. But this matter need not be considered further. It is enough for the present purpose that, whether pure competition or some degree of monopoly is present, in all ordinary circumstances the demand schedule for labour as a whole stands higher, the higher the demand schedule for output as a whole is standing ; which means in effect, the larger is money income or outlay.[1]

[1] It has been suggested by Mr. Harrod that in a régime of imperfect competition the demand for the output of a representative centre of production is likely to become less elastic the larger is aggregate real income.

II

On the assumption set out in the opening paragraph, that money rate of wages and money demand schedule are independent of one another, it is plain that, for any given state of the demand schedule for labour, there is some rate of money wage in respect of which the quantity of labour demanded is exactly equal to the (given) quantity that is offering itself for work; and that for any given rate of money wage there is some state of the demand schedule for labour in respect of which this will be true. When the wage rate and demand schedule are thus adjusted, the market is exactly cleared, so that there are no would-be wage-earners without work and no vacancies which employers desire, but are unable, to fill. When wage rate and demand schedule are not thus adjusted, the maladjustment may be of such a sort that more labour is desired than is available and there is a gap consisting of unfilled vacancies; or it may be of such a sort that less labour is demanded than is available and there is a gap consisting of unemployed work-people. It is only the second of these types of maladjustment that is for the moment of interest to us. We may attribute it indifferently to the wage rate being too high, the demand schedule being taken as given, or, the wage rate being taken as given, to the demand schedule being too low. Wage rate and demand schedule are like the two blades of Marshall's scissors, neither of which can be said in an absolute sense to do the cutting but either of which can be said to do it if we suppose the other to be held steady.

If this is so, and if it becomes less elastic with sufficient sharpness, the statement of the text will not be true. There is, however, at least as much to be said against as in favour of Mr. Harrod's suggestion (cf. my *Employment and Equilibrium*, pp. 47-9). In practice Mr. Harrod does not deny that, with a stable demand schedule for the product of labour, a rise in wage rates cannot normally carry with it rising employment (cf. *Economic Journal*, December 1943, p. 341).

III

With the demand schedule taken as given, the following propositions may be asserted. First, for all wage rates not greater than the rate adjusted to the demand schedule in the way described above full employment will prevail. Thus for rates below this adjusted rate differences in rates do not carry with them any differences in unemployment. Secondly, for wage rates above the adjusted rate unemployment will always be larger, the higher the wage rate, up to the point — if there is such a point [1] — at which everybody is unemployed. Thirdly, given the excess of the actual wage rate above the adjusted rate, unemployment will be larger the more elastic, over the relevant range, is the demand for labour. For a more elastic demand schedule means one in which the quantity demanded falls by a higher percentage in response to a given (small) percentage increase in price asked. All these propositions are, I think, self-evident. With the wage rate taken as given, there are two companion propositions corresponding to the two first of the above. First, for levels of the money demand schedule for labour not lower than the adjusted level, full employment will prevail at whatever level the demand schedule for labour may stand. Secondly, for levels of the money demand schedule below the adjusted level, unemployment will always be larger the lower the money demand schedule stands, till that level is reached in respect of which everybody is unemployed.[2] These propositions also are self-evident.

[1] If the demand curve is a hyperbola, rectangular or otherwise, obviously there will not be such a point.
[2] In the text it is tacitly assumed that, if demand schedule A is higher than demand schedule B in respect of some quantities of labour, it must be higher in respect of all quantities. For cases in which this assumption does not hold, the concept of higher and lower is ambiguous.

CHAPTER III

WAGE RATES AND UNEMPLOYMENT

IF, as was supposed in the last chapter, the money demand schedule for labour were in fact wholly independent of the rate of money wages, it would follow that, when employment was less than full, it could always be increased and, if so desired, brought up to full by making the money wage rate lower. But the above supposition does not fit the facts, and further discussion is, therefore, needed.

We may conveniently begin by setting on one side a consideration that for the present purpose is of minor importance. Our problem refers to connections between demands for labour and levels of wage rates taken by themselves, not accompanied by expectations of future changes in wage rates. It is well known that a low level for the price of tea, if it is expected to be followed shortly by a still lower level, may be associated with a lower demand schedule and less purchases of tea than a high level expected to maintain itself; for the expectation of a future fall in price may cause buyers to hold off from the market for the time being. Exactly the same thing may happen if wages in general, while low, are expected soon to become lower. We are not here concerned with this class of reaction. We have to envisage two simple alternatives: a wage rate, W, expected to be stable and a wage rate, mW (where m may be either greater or less than 1), also expected to be stable.

With this understanding let us pass to the main issue. This is best approached indirectly. It has been argued that the Ford Motor Company in the United States found advantage in paying high wages to their work-people because this enabled those work-people to become purchasers of Ford cars. That is to say, high wages for Ford work-people push up the money demand schedule for Ford cars; which implies that indirectly the money demand schedule for the services of the work-people making these cars is also pushed up. Plainly, however, the proportion of any ordinary worker's wage that he spends on the article made by the industry in which he is himself engaged is too small to allow this effect to be other than negligible. Broadly speaking, the rate of wages paid in any industry, *a fortiori* in any individual firm in an industry, has no effect on the money demand schedule for the commodity that the industry produces and, consequently, no effect on the derived money demand schedule for the labour engaged in making it.

A careless reasoner, having satisfied himself on this point, may be tempted to suppose that what is thus true for any single industry taken by itself must also be true of the whole body of industries taken together, and so to conclude without more ado that differences in wage rates over industry as a whole necessarily leave the money demand schedule for labour in the aggregate unaffected. But this inference involves a fallacy. It ignores the possibility that higher (or lower) wage rates in industry A may react on the demand schedule for labour in industries B, C, and D. It is thus on a par with the argument that, because any one man, by picking pockets, can enrich himself individually, therefore all men collectively, by picking pockets, can do this. The relation between wage rates as a whole and employment as a whole cannot be settled by studying separately the relations between wage rates and employment in no matter how many individual industries. Another method is required.

It is to be expected on the face of things that with different types of monetary arrangement the relations between money wage rates and the money demand schedule for labour in the aggregate will be different.

Hence no generalisation of universal validity can be looked for. We must begin by examining some single precisely defined type of monetary arrangement, enquire what will happen if that type is established, and then proceed to build on the foundations so laid. The type of arrangement which best lends itself to this purpose is one in which the quantity of money — currency, bank money and, if we will, overdraft facilities — in the hands of the public (and Government authorities) is rigidly fixed.

Contemplating this arrangement, we may regard the fixed stock of money as made up of two parts, an active part and a passive part — active balances and idle balances. The active part of the total stock we may suppose to circulate from income to income at a fixed velocity depending upon business technique and private habits, so that the interval between successive appearances as income of a representative unit of money is, say, c months; which implies that aggregate money income per annum is $\frac{12}{c}$ times the stock of active money. The passive part of the total stock, on the other hand, does not circulate at all. Of course, the total stock, which consists largely of bank deposits, is not divided up into physically distinguishable units of which some are active and some passive. But this fact is not material. It is perfectly proper for us to proceed *as if* different units of money were physically distinguishable; for it is the comparative sizes of the two parts of the money stock, not its individual elements, that are relevant to the analysis.

Plainly, then, a transfer of x units of money from the passive to the active part of the stock entails that annual money income after the change exceeds what it was before by $\frac{12}{c}$ times x units. In more general terms, the larger is the active as compared with the passive stock, the larger aggregate money income will be; which is the same thing as saying, the higher the money demand schedule for output as a whole will be.

Now the proportion between active and passive money depends on many factors : tradition, custom, taste, and so on. Among them one potent factor is the expected rate of return from real investment, *which, in the stable conditions we are here postulating, is equivalent to the rate of interest.*[1] The higher this is, the less willing people will be to allow their money to lie passive, the keener to employ it to set the wheel of profit rolling. It follows that, the better the prospective return from an increment of real investment, and so the higher the rate of interest, the larger the active part of the money stock will be. Hence the larger aggregate money income will be, and so the higher the money demand schedule for output as a whole.

We have seen that the demand schedule for labour as a whole is derived from the demand schedule for output as a whole; and, without going into detail, we may for our purposes reasonably assume that the level of money wages does not affect the money demand schedule for labour unless it also affects the money demand schedule for output as a whole; and that, if it affects either of these schedules, it affects both of them in the same sense. Thus, more specifically, differences in money wage rates entail no differences in the money demand schedule for labour unless they carry with them differences in the rate of interest ; but, if they do that, they do entail differences in the money demand schedule for labour ; higher interest being associated with a higher, lower with a lower demand schedule. This is the clue that we have to follow up.

Let us then suppose ourselves to be confronted with two situations, in both of which the surrounding circumstances are the same, but in one the money wage rate is lower than in the other. We have to enquire what this

[1] Cf. *post*, Chap. V. paragraph 2.

will entail as regards the relation between the associated money demand schedules for labour. It is easy to see that in the situation with the lower wage rate the money demand schedule must stand somewhat lower than in the other. For, if it did not, there being more employment and so more real income, people would be more willing to save, and the rate of interest would, therefore, be lower. But, as we know from the preceding paragraph, for the rate of interest to be lower *entails* the money demand schedule for labour being lower. But how much lower must the money demand schedule for labour be? Can it be lower to such an extent that employment in the low-wage situation is as small as it is in the other situation? To settle this issue let us suppose that the answer is yes. Then employment, and so real income, and so the amount of saving offered, and so the rate of interest are the same in the two situations. It follows that the money demand schedule for labour must also be the same. This contradicts our initial assumption. Hence, we conclude, in the low-wage situation the money demand schedule for labour will be lower than in the other situation, but not enough lower to prevent employment in the low wage situation from being larger than in the other.

The preceding analysis has been concerned with a monetary arrangement in which the stock of money is held constant. But no actual monetary arrangement is of this kind. On the contrary, the stock of money is always subject to alteration. Hence, how the demand schedule for labour is related to differences in the money rate of wage depends in part on the way in which the rate of wage affects the size of the *total* stock of money. There are a number of different types of arrangement. It is natural to begin with what we may call perhaps the normal type, where the banking system acts on ordinary business principles and is prepared to allow outstanding loans, and so deposits — the stock of money — to be larger, the higher is the rate of interest. With this system higher rates of interest may be expected to promote larger active stocks of money, not only by making the proportion of the total stock that is active larger but also by making the total stock itself larger ; and conversely for lower rates of interest. Hence, with this type of monetary arrangement, a low money wage rate will be responsible for a more extensive lowering of the money demand schedule for labour than the arrangement previously described. But, for the reasons given in the last paragraph, it is impossible for the demand schedule to be so far lower in the low-wage situation as to prevent employment from being larger in that situation than in the other.

Turn to a quite different type of monetary arrangement. In the pre-1914 period the monies of the leading nations were linked together by the international gold standard or by the variation of it known as the gold exchange standard. Under this system the sizes of the total stocks of money in the several countries were so regulated that the rates of exchange between their several monies were held stable ; which implied that the prices in these monies, at all events of goods entering into international trade, kept more or less in step. Under this plan it is evident that a lower money wage rate in one country, by cheapening output there, would stimulate exports and discourage imports, and so bring about an influx of gold and make the stock of money larger. Thus low wage rates would cause the money demand schedule for labour to stand higher than it would have done if the stock of money had been fixed. Employment in a low-wage situation will, therefore, exceed employment in a high-wage situation more markedly than it would have done with a fixed total stock of money. The same thing is true in a country whose monetary system is tied to the money systems of other large countries through more or less informal policies directed to maintaining some measure of exchange stability — as, for example, under the inter-war tripartite agreement between the United Kingdom, the United States, and France.

If a country's monetary arrangements are not linked in any way to those of other countries or if, as in war-time, the normal consequences of formal linkages (*e.g.* the war-time pegging of the sterling dollar exchange) are overridden by Governmental control of imports and exports, a system *may* be established under which differences in wage rates react on the demand schedule for labour sufficiently to prevent low wage rates from being associated with *any* more employment than high wage rates would be. Experience has shown that in periods of total war, should wage-earners succeed in forcing up money rates of wages, the Government, rather than allow man-power to go unused, will cause new money to be created and will force it into the active part of the stock in sufficient amount to absorb nearly everybody into work at the higher wage. It is plainly possible for a monetary setting to exist in which *reductions* in wage rates are associated with analogous reactions on the demand schedule for labour. Nor is it difficult to see what the essential character of that setting is. It is that the money rate of interest is held back from falling when money wage rates are reduced. The argument of the middle of p. 14 showed that a contraction in money wage rates cannot carry with it an equal proportionate cut in money income, and so also in the money demand for labour, unless the rate of interest " stays put " ; and in the conditions there postulated the rate of interest cannot stay put. If, however, it does stay put, the contraction in money wage rates not only may, but necessarily will, entail an equi-proportionate contraction in money income and the money demand for labour. There is no reason for the amount of real investment to be altered ; therefore no reason for real income to be altered ; and, therefore, finally no reason for employ-

WAGE RATES AND UNEMPLOYMENT

ment to be altered. Thus the level of employment will be what it will be irrespective of what happens to the money rate of wages.

What has been said enables us to conclude in a general way that, unless a country's monetary system operates in the manner that has just been described, the establishment and maintenance of lower rates of wages, though this is likely to cause the demand schedule for labour to stand lower than it would do with higher rates, will not cause it to stand so much lower as to prevent the volume of employment from being larger. On the contrary, in all ordinary circumstances, so long as employment is less than full, by permitting a lower level of money wage rates we shall cause employment to be larger and the lapse from full employment to be smaller than they would be if a higher level were maintained. It would thus seem that, subject to the exception noted above, full employment could be secured by an appropriate manipulation of money wage rates. Moreover, a once-for-all manipulation would suffice. It would not be necessary to undertake any process of progressive wage reductions.

CHAPTER IV

THOROUGH-GOING COMPETITION AMONG WAGE-EARNERS

IF thorough-going competition prevailed among wage-earners, it is evident that, in the conditions supposed in the last chapter, *save only those indicated in the penultimate paragraph*, for any given state of demand wage rates would be adjusted in such a way as to secure full employment. For, so long as anybody is unemployed, he will offer himself for employment and, in order to secure it, will beat wages down — if beating down is necessary — until it becomes profitable for employers to engage the services of everybody who is offering them.[1] This argument, it should be observed, is independent of whether employers compete freely with one another for purchasers of their goods or — some or all of them — exercise some degree of monopolistic power. The rate of wages that secures full employment is, indeed, likely to be lower in the latter case than in the former; but in either case employment will be full.

Reasoning of the above type is easily extended to cover

[1] It may perhaps be thought that, if wages are paid in kind and if over the relevant range constant returns prevail, in such wise that the marginal productivity, and so — in competitive conditions — the real demand price per unit of labour, is the same in respect of a series of different quantities, the quantity of employment will be indeterminate. That is not correct. It is true that in these conditions equality of wage rate asked for and demand price does not determine the quantity of labour demanded at a specific amount. Employers are equally willing to take any amount in respect of which this equality holds. But thorough-going competition among wage-earners *does* determine this, requiring it to be equal to the quantity of labour on offer. More generally, for a demand schedule to be represented by a horizontal line does not entail indeterminateness in quantity bought unless, by some miracle, the supply schedule over the relevant part of its length is represented by another coincidental horizontal line.

THOROUGH-GOING COMPETITION

the more general case in which labour is not perfectly mobile among centres of production, but specified numbers of work-people are tied to the several centres as the result, maybe, of historical accident. Here too thorough-going competition among wage-earners would secure that full employment was established everywhere except in centres where, in order to establish it, wage rates would need to be nil or negative. We might, indeed, say that, apart from State intervention, full employment would be established in these centres also because the superfluous wage-earners, having no earnings, would die! There would be full employment, but divergent wage rates. Thus from a formal, though not, of course, from a practical point of view, the proposition that thorough-going competition among wage-earners entails full employment is always valid except in the special conditions to which attention has been drawn.

CHAPTER V

THE CLASSICAL VIEW

THE foregoing analysis has been on the lines of classical political economy. The architects of that discipline never had any doubt that, provided only thorough-going competition exists among wage-earners, there must be a tendency towards full employment, and, apart from changes and frictions, there must actually be full employment. This implies that in stable conditions, apart from friction, imperfect mobility and so on, the establishment of a sufficiently low rate of money wages would carry with it full employment in *all* circumstances. In the last paragraph but one of Chapter III it was indicated that, with a certain type of monetary setting, lower wage rates carry with them correspondingly lower demands for labour, so that, if we start from a situation in which employment is less than full, it is impossible to make it full by establishing lower rates of wages. Thus the classical view needs to be qualified. In this chapter the exact nature of the qualification and its significance for practice will be examined.

Two preliminary matters must be made clear. First, stable conditions imply an expectation that the relative values of all different kinds of commodities will be substantially [1] the same for a considerable period in the future as they are now. This in turn implies that the rates of interest on loans cannot be different when expressed in terms of different things, but that the money rate and every kind of commodity rate must be the same. Thus

[1] Not *exactly* the same, because we do not exclude from our "stable conditions", as we should have to do from a stationary state, a slow growth in the stock of capital.

THE CLASSICAL VIEW

we can always speak simply of *the* rate of interest without distinguishing between the money rate and any kind or kinds of real rate.

Secondly, we have to define precisely the sense in which two governing words are to be used. These words are investment and saving. Real investment is that part of real income which consists in net additions to the stock of capital; *i.e.* it is real income minus real consumption. Real saving is the excess of real income over real consumption. It follows that (aggregate) real saving is by definition equivalent to (aggregate) real investment. Money income, money investment, and money saving are the money values of the above real items; which, of course, implies that (aggregate) money saving is equivalent to (aggregate) money investment. Some writers prefer to give other meanings to these words. It is important, therefore, if confusion is to be avoided, that the sense in which they are used here should be borne carefully in mind.

These preliminaries being disposed of, consider first normal conditions, in which the rate of interest is standing well above the minimum level at which it *can* stand. It is open to the authorities, if they choose, to control monetary and banking processes with the deliberate purpose of preventing this rate from being reduced no matter what happens to the rate of money wages. If they do this and if we start with a situation in which employment is, by some accident, less than full, it is, as we have seen, impossible to make it full by establishing lower rates of wages. But is such a policy at all likely to be pursued in fact ? When, in the hope of lessening unemployment, work people agree to accept lower rates of wages, why should the banking system desire, and, if it does desire, why should it be allowed by the Government, to adopt a monetary technique the effect of which will simply be to prevent them from achieving their purpose ? There can be no reason save either stupidity or spite; and there is no ground whatever to expect the monetary authorities to be stupid, let alone spiteful. We need not, therefore, I suggest, take this possibility seriously into account.

There is, however, a second and much more important case to be considered. Since people, if they choose, can hold their own money at practically no cost, the money rate of interest cannot be significantly negative; probably for technical reasons it cannot stand permanently at less than a small positive rate. Suppose that after a long period of peace such large additions to capital stock have been made and inventive genius has been so sluggish that no openings offering a net positive return to investment in excess of this minimum rate of interest exist. Of course, the lack of private demand may be offset by special action on the part of the State, which is free, if it desires to do so, to invest to any extent at a nil or even high negative rate of return. If the State acts so it can prevent aggregate investment from falling far enough to drive the rate of interest down to the minimum. But, if it does not, the rate will fall to that. The rate then being at its minimum, not only *can be prevented* from being pushed down further by a caprice of the authorities, but *is automatically so prevented* by *force majeure*. It is impossible for contractions in money income brought about by reductions in money wage rates (or in any other way) to lead to reductions in it. Thus the type of relation between money income and money rate of interest contemplated at the end of the last chapter *must* be realised. This entails that, if we once get into a position where employment is less than full, the establishment of lower rates of wages cannot enable us to get out of it. The classical thesis, that thorough-going competition among wage-earners creates a tendency towards full employment, is not valid in these conditions.

Lord Keynes's alternative story is broadly as follows.

THE CLASSICAL VIEW

When, through a failure of profitable openings for investment, the rate of interest has been forced down to the minimum, it is probable that people will want to supply some savings (investment) for reasons of prestige, security, and so on, even though none are demanded. So long as there is an excess in what they want to supply for investment above what is demanded for it, they will try to satisfy their desire by drawing money out of circulation to hold it in stockings or in savings deposits. Thus there must come about a continuous withdrawal of more and more money from circulation and a resultant continuous fall in the size of aggregate money income. If money wage rates do not fall this leads directly to reduced employment; if they do fall, since the cuts in wages set up equivalent further cuts in money income, it still leads to this, the only difference being that money income comes down faster. This downward process does not, however, go on for ever, because, as employment falls, real income falls too, and, as real income falls, people, being poorer, do not desire to make such large savings. Thus ultimately there is no longer an excess in the amount of what they want to save or invest above the amount that industrialists require. At this point the downward process stops and there is established a new low-level equilibrium, with employment much less than full.

In my opinion this is not an entirely satisfactory account of what may be expected to happen. Suppose that, when the original equilibrium is disturbed by opportunities for profitable investment being contracted in the way we have described and, in consequence, money income goes crashing downwards, money wage rates crash downwards parallel with it. It is true that, since the rate of interest does not fall, the cuts in money wage rates entail equivalent proportionate cuts in money income and the money demand for labour. But the several actions and reactions are presumably separated by time-lags. Hence, it would seem, though, owing to the inevitable lag in the first wage reduction, employment must be cut down, it will not be cut down progressively. The pursuer will *be* behind the pursued because he has got a worse start, but will not afterwards fall further behind him. Hence Lord Keynes's low-level equilibrium will not be attained. Nevertheless, the downward process *will* presently be arrested. For the extent to which people desire to save at a given rate of return depends, not only on the size of their real income, but also on the amount of capital wealth, as valued in terms of the goods contained in that real income, that they have already accumulated. The larger this is, the less keen they will be to save. But, since, after employment and the scale of real income have ceased falling, money income continues to fall, prices also must continue to fall. Hence, as valued in terms of income goods, such accumulated wealth as is embodied in the stock of money — and also in certain other non-reproducible types of durable goods that are specially attractive as stores of value — grows continuously larger. Eventually a stage must be reached at which this development — not a progressive fall in real income — reduces people's desire to save sufficiently to allow a new equilibrium to establish itself. This is not, indeed, a full employment equilibrium, because the initial wage reaction is sure to be delayed, but one which may well be much nearer to that than Lord Keynes's low level equilibrium.

What has been said in the last two paragraphs is controversial. It is, therefore, important to realise that for practice the issue is not a very important one. Popular writers often assert quite generally that saving is inimical to employment because it leads to a contraction in money income, and so, even if there is thorough-going competition among wage-earners, to that breakdown of employment which the critics of the classical view envisage. From this they infer that employment will be increased

THE CLASSICAL VIEW

if income is transferred from rich people to poor people, since poor people are likely to save a smaller proportion of their income. But it is only in conditions where opportunities for real investment are insufficient *on the whole* — not merely during the down-phase of a trade cycle — to absorb all the savings which people wish to make that there is any tendency for money income to contract in such a way as to evoke the situation we have been discussing. Such conditions, of course, *might* exist. There is, however, little reason to think that they ever have existed. Nor, with the dire need for new capital creations which is bound to be felt after this war is over, can we reasonably expect that they will exist, at all events until many years have elapsed.

The final result of this discussion is to suggest that, though there are subtleties of theory which the classicists did not envisage, for broad practical purposes their conclusion was correct. In stable conditions, apart from frictions, immobility and so on, thorough-going competition among wage-earners would ensure the establishment and maintenance of full employment except in circumstances which we are very unlikely to meet with in fact. True, in some conditions it might not be able to do this except at the cost of forcing money (not real) wage rates down to a very low level. If these conditions were realised, it might well happen that popular resentment or Government decree would prevent wage rates from establishing themselves at the required rate. Should this happen, however, thorough-going competition among wage-earners would have been interdicted; and it is no part of the classical view that, if that were done, there would be a tendency for full employment to establish itself.

CHAPTER VI

THE ACTUAL LEVEL OF WAGE RATES

EXPERIENCE shows that, at all events in this country, strong forces are at work tending to set money rates of wages higher in relation to the state of demand and the number of applicants for work than they would stand if thorough-going competition among wage-earners did in fact exist, and higher, therefore, than permit of the maintenance of full employment. Let us consider briefly the character of these forces, remembering that stable conditions are being postulated, so that we are not interested in influences that depend upon the demand for labour in the aggregate being subject to fluctuations. How, then, are wage rates actually settled? In modern conditions in such a country as England they are settled in the main separately in various groups of industries either by collective bargaining between organisations of wage-earners and organisations of employers or, where organisation is inadequate, by officially controlled trade boards. Of course, these agencies in their decisions have regard to the general state of the demand for labour; they will have no wish to set wage rates so high that half the people of the country are thrown out of work. Nevertheless, there is reason to believe that they do not have regard to demand conditions in such degree as would be necessary to secure, as thorough-going competition would do, the establishment of full employment.

Thus, consider the attitude of a group of work-people engaged in collective bargaining. We are not for the present interested in differences between various occupations and places. Nothing, therefore, need be said about the circumstances that render some groups of work-people better able

THE ACTUAL LEVEL OF WAGE RATES

to press for high wage rates than others. We are concerned only with influences of a general character. Prominent among these is the fact that, even though higher wage rates entailed so much more unemployment than lower wage rates that the aggregate earnings of all work-people, employed and unemployed together, were lower — which need not, of course, be the case, — work-people's organisations might, nevertheless, prefer the higher wage rates. They might do this either through a failure to realise the effects of the higher rates on employment or as a deliberate act of policy undertaken with a full understanding of the facts ; and that even in a community where the State assumed no responsibility for safeguarding the interests of unemployed persons. In a community where the State does assume this responsibility the inducement to wage-earners to try to push up wage rates, in spite of any tendency the high rates may have to promote unemployment, is much stronger ; for in these conditions the cost of looking after the unemployed is, in the main, taken out of their hands. Now, as everybody knows, in Great Britain and in a number of other countries the State does assume responsibility in that matter, contriving, through an elaborate machinery, that unemployed persons shall receive maintenance pay, the funds for which are provided in part by compulsory contributions from employers and employed and in part out of Government resources, that is by the taxpayers as a whole. Every improvement in the rate of benefit paid to unemployed persons, and every increase in the length of period over which benefit is paid under a national system of social security, lessens the extent to which fear of consequential unemployment deters trade unions from exerting pressure for higher and higher wages.

In industries where wage-earners are too badly organised to operate a system of collective bargaining effectively it is usual in this country for trade boards, containing some independent members appointed by the State, to be set up to fix minimum wage rates. These bodies are, of course, guided in their decisions by a consideration of what is happening to wages in the general body of industry. Humanitarian sentiment also plays a part in their deliberations, operating through the notion of " a reasonable standard of living ". People's ideas as to what this is are affected by the scale of the provision that the State has decided to make for unemployed persons, destitute persons, and even criminals in prison. The " reasonable standard " for free wage-earners must clearly be superior to the highest of these standards. In general the upward pressure on wage rates to push them above what thorough-going competition would provide may be presumed to operate where trade boards rule at least as strongly as it does where wages are regulated by collective bargaining.

A further consideration has to be borne in mind, which is relevant to both these types of regulation. The decisions taken refer in the main to standard rates of wages for workers in any class who are of normal efficiency for that class. Though arrangements are often made to allow workers suffering from some definite and clearly marked disability to be engaged at less than standard rates, it is not easy to make such arrangements for workers who, though not so suffering, are, nevertheless, of abnormally low capacity. In occupations where piece wages are paid this does not greatly matter ; though even here a man who works half as quickly as another is not worth to the employer half the other's wage, because, besides working less quickly himself, he also causes the machine on which he is engaged to work less quickly. When time wages are paid it is obvious that, with a uniform standard of wage per hour, inferior men are being paid at a higher rate per unit of efficiency than others. Hence, even when for these others the rates are not higher than thorough-going competition would bring about, in view of the

THE ACTUAL LEVEL OF WAGE RATES

difficulty of making adjustments in the standard rate to fit individual capacities, it is very likely that the rates ruling for inferior workers will be higher than that. So far as they are concerned, there is a special pressure on wage rates over and above that to which the general body of wage rates is exposed.

In view of these considerations we might fairly expect that in a country such as England, even if all the simplifying conditions set out at the beginning of Chapter II were present, wage rates would be found standing too high in relation to the state of demand and the number of persons seeking work to allow of full employment being attained.

CHAPTER VII

THE DISTRIBUTION OF WAGE RATES AND UNEMPLOYMENT

FROM what has been said it is clear that in stable conditions, where tendencies have room to work themselves out, with thorough-going competition among wage-earners, if labour is perfectly free to move among centres of production, there will be both full employment and equal wage rates everywhere; while, if labour is not perfectly free to move and there is thorough-going competition, there will be full employment but unequal wage rates. There remains the case in which labour is perfectly free to move and there is not thorough-going competition. Obviously in this case there will be no tendency towards full employment. Nor is it either necessary or likely that wage rates will be equal everywhere. Thus a new problem arises. The average rate of wage over all the centres (namely the sum of the products of wage rate multiplied by number of persons employed in each centre divided by aggregate number of persons employed) being supposed given, we have to enquire how aggregate employment is related to the distribution of the several different wage rates. This problem is most conveniently tackled in two stages. First, I shall consider how, with different arrangements of wage rates, the aggregate quantities of labour demanded are related to each other. Secondly, I shall bring into account the fact that, with some wage arrangements, there may be unfilled vacancies in some centres, so that the aggregate quantity of *labour employed* is less in a greater or less degree than the aggregate quantity of *labour demanded*.[1]

[1] It may perhaps be objected to this procedure that the quantity of labour demanded at a given wage rate in one centre will be different according

WAGE RATES AND UNEMPLOYMENT

I

The quantity of labour demanded in any centre at a given wage rate does not depend simply on that wage rate, but partly also on the wage rates that rule in other centres. For, in general, the wage rate of one centre affects the quantity of money spent on the output of the centre and so, aggregate money income being given, the amount available for spending on the output of other centres. Thus the demand for labour in one centre in respect of a given wage rate there can only be said to have such-and-such an elasticity on the assumption that wage rates elsewhere are given. Hence, when two situations differ in respect of *a number of wage rates*, the percentage differences in the quantities of labour demanded at the several centres are not simply equal to the percentage differences in wage rates multiplied by the appropriate elasticities, as calculated for each centre on the assumption that wage rates elsewhere are given. Nevertheless, it is *probable* that, if the elasticity in the above sense of the demand for labour at centre A is greater than the corresponding elasticity at centre B, a given proportionate change in wage will entail a larger proportionate change as there are or are not unfilled vacancies in other centres. If that were so, we could not properly take the aggregate quantity of labour demanded as determined by the set of wage rates, and then obtain the aggregate quantity of employment by subtracting from this the number of unfilled vacancies. But in fact that is not so. For suppose that at a given centre one hundred men are employed. There is then a determinate output of product there, for which, all other wages and all prices being given, purchasers are ready to pay a given aggregate sum, leaving the difference between this sum and aggregate money income (supposed fixed) available for spending on other kinds of goods. This aggregate sum is the same whether the wage rate in our centre is such that a hundred men in that centre are demanded there and there are no unfilled vacancies, or such that more than a hundred men are demanded there and there are some unfilled vacancies. The two cases differ in that in the former a larger share of the purchase price of our centre's output goes to the wage-earners engaged there and a smaller share to the non-wage-earners. The *total* purchase price is the same in both cases; and, consequently, the demand for other products, and so for the labour engaged in making other products, is also the same in both.

in the quantity of labour demanded at A than at B. Granted this, we are able to infer that, if, the average level of wages per person employed being held constant, wages stand above the average in centres where the demand is less elastic and below it in centres where the demand is more elastic, the aggregate quantity of labour demanded in all the centres will be larger than it would be if wage rates everywhere stood at the average level; and conversely.[1] This generalisation, though not easy to establish or even to set out precisely without the help of symbols, is in general accordance with common sense and is not likely to be seriously resisted.

Now, as we have seen, unless thorough-going competition among wage-earners prevails, there is no reason, even with labour perfectly mobile, to expect rates of wages to be equal in different centres. In some centres, or groups of centres constituting occupations, wage-earners will be in a much stronger bargaining position than in others. I do not merely mean that, as between two groups of wage-earners, if in the one the percentage of unemployment is high and in the other low, the latter group is likely, other things being equal, to be stronger. With *equal* unemployment percentages different groups will be of different strengths. Thus those with well-organised trade unions and large financial resources will be specially strong. So also, and this is what matters here, will those for whose services demand is highly inelastic — because, for example, there is no foreign competition with their products, — so that a given percentage increase in wage rates would only entail a small percentage decrease in the number of workers demanded.

It is reasonable to expect, then, that wage rates will vary in different occupations more or less with the bargaining strength of the several groups of wage-earners over against their employers. There is, therefore, some

[1] Compare my *Theory of Unemployment*, pp. 264-5.

presumption that, on the whole, wage rates will tend to be relatively high in occupations where the demand for labour is relatively inelastic.

An important consequence follows. Provided that the quantity of labour demanded and the quantity of employment coincide everywhere, the kind of inequality of wages that we may look to find in practice is likely to make aggregate employment larger, and so aggregate unemployment smaller, than it would be with uniform wage rates of the same average size.

II

We thus come to the second stage of our analysis, that touching the relation between aggregate quantity of labour employed and aggregate quantity demanded. Obviously, if the numbers of persons seeking work at the several occupations were determined merely by historical accident, nothing significant could be said about this. But in conditions supposed to be stable labour may be expected to have sufficient — so to speak — long-term mobility to ensure that the numbers of persons attached to the several occupations are adjusted to the comparative prospects of earnings that they offer, or, if we prefer it, to what we may call for brevity the actuarial attractiveness of different occupations. This conception needs to be worked out and clarified.

In a community where no provision is made for unemployed workers actuarial attractiveness is measured for any centre by the wage rate — elements of net advantage other than the wage rate may be ignored — ruling there multiplied by the mean percentage, over good and bad times together, of employment (*i.e.* 100 less the percentage of unemployment) ruling there. In a community in which benefit or allowance is paid to unemployed work-people the actuarial attractiveness of the several centres is better regarded as measuring the prospect of *receipts*, account being taken of unemployment benefit as well as of the prospects of earnings in them. It is evident that the actuarial attractiveness in this sense differs less, as between centres of large and small mean unemployment, than actuarial attractiveness in the other sense does. For our purpose, however, we need not for the most part trouble to distinguish between the two senses.

The actuarial attractiveness of an occupation does not necessarily represent its attractive power ; for it does not necessarily measure the prospect of earnings offered to newcomers. It only does this if a newcomer may reasonably consider his chances of employment as good, or nearly as good, as those of a man who is already attached to the occupation. In occupations where applicants are either accepted and given what in effect amount to life jobs or rejected altogether, as happens in the higher branches of the Civil Service, he cannot do this. However high the wage rates in such jobs might be, nobody except people actually employed in them would become attached to them — hanging about the doors of the Treasury on the look-out for a vacancy ! Consequently, their actuarial attractiveness, namely wage rate multiplied by proportion of attached men employed, might be very much higher than elsewhere and yet no attractive force whatever might be exerted by them to draw people from elsewhere. This way of engaging labour is not, however, used in ordinary industries. A newcomer into the orbit of such an industry may reckon on his prospects, not perhaps immediately but in all events after a little while, being as good as those of any other man of similar capacity. In these circumstances actuarial attractiveness does, *prima facie*, correspond to attractive power.

This *prima facie* appearance is not, indeed, to be fully trusted. For men are less — or more — than mathematical machines. Thus in sweepstakes and lotteries many people, impressed with the possibility of a large prize, will gladly pay much more for a ticket than the value of the prize multiplied by the probability of winning it, which is the actuarial worth of a ticket. In the case of earnings prospects there is a further complication. The elements really relevant to choice are future wage rates and future chances of employment, while the only elements that can be known are past and present wage rates and unemployment percentages. Moreover, the ordinary would-be employee is frequently ill-informed even about these elements. Thus he may pay too much attention to one of the elements and too little to the other. For example, fifty years ago, when information about employment was much less readily accessible than it is to-day, it may well be that, in choosing their crafts, people paid little attention to it as compared with rates of wages, Now, on the other hand, everybody is employment-conscious — the problem of employment has largely superseded in the public mind the problem of wages —; so that, it may well be, insufficient attention is paid to wage rates. Still there can be little doubt that, as between different occupations, greater actuarial attractiveness is more likely than not to be associated with greater attractive power, and is much more likely than not to be so associated if the difference between occupations in actuarial attractiveness is considerable.

This implies that, when, for men of similar quality, different rates of wages are established in different occupations — or in different places — there is a force at work tending to make would-be wage-earners attach themselves to the several occupations in such relative numbers that in occupations of high wage rates there is a larger percentage of unemployment than in occupations of low wage rates ; the " proper " adjustment being one in which actuarial attractiveness is everywhere the same.

Granted, then, that wage rates tend to be above the average in occupations where the demand for labour is of less than average elasticity and below it in occupations of converse type, it follows that men will tend to attach themselves to the former type of occupation in abnormally large and to the latter in abnormally small numbers. This does not necessarily entail the existence of unfilled vacancies anywhere. If wage rates are sufficiently high, there will, on the contrary, be some unemployed men everywhere. In this case the aggregate quantity of labour employed will be equal to the aggregate quantity demanded; and there is, therefore, a presumption that aggregate employment will be larger and unemployment smaller than it would have been with the same average wage rate but with all individual rates equal.

But the condition required for this, that, as we may say, there is enough unemployment to go round, is not always satisfied. Thus, suppose that the wage rates in occupation I and occupation II are respectively W and mW (where m is less than 1), and the quantities of labour demanded at these wage rates in the two occupations are a and b, while the total number of wage-earners is N. In order that the number of wage-earners attached to occupation II may be greater than or equal to the number demanded there, the rule of equal actuarial attractiveness requires that the number attached to occupation I must be greater than or equal to $1/m$ times the number demanded there. Hence, in order that the number attached to each occupation may be equal to or greater than the number demanded in each, N must equal to or exceed $\left(\dfrac{a}{m}+b\right)$. If the wage rates, W and mW, are such that this condition is satisfied, there are no unfilled vacancies anywhere; there is enough unemployment to go round. But, if the wage rates are so low that the condition $N => \left(\dfrac{a}{m}+b\right)$ is not satisfied, there is not enough unemployment to go round. A system under which wage rates are higher in occupations of inelastic than in occupations of elastic demand need not in these conditions carry with it more aggregate employment, and, therefore, less aggregate unemployment, than one in which the average level of wage rates is the same but rates are uniform everywhere. Whether it *will* do so or not cannot be determined in general, but depends on the detailed circumstances of each particular case.

III

As a rider to what has been said, we can easily see that, with non-uniform wage rates, where the rule of equal actuarial attractiveness operates, no all-round equi-proportional cut in wage rates, however large, will serve to make employment full, *i.e.* to reduce unemployment to nothing. It is impossible to do this except by violating the rule and dragging away to work elsewhere men who have attached themselves, in unemployment, to high-wage occupations. In this respect a system under which labour is distributed in accordance with the rule of equal actuarial attractiveness stands in sharp contrast to one in which it is distributed arbitrarily in a once-for-all way. For in that case an equi-proportional cut in all wage rates (not offset by an equivalent contraction in the money demand schedule for labour) necessarily increases employment in any occupation where it is not already full; which implies, apart from the special case where negative or nil rates would be needed, that a sufficiently large all-round cut could always evoke full employment.

CHAPTER VIII

THE DEMAND FOR LABOUR AND UNEMPLOYMENT

LET us now revert to the case in which a single uniform rate of wages rules everywhere and labour is perfectly mobile among the several centres of production. If the money rate of wages were wholly independent of the state of the money demand schedule for labour, it would follow that, when employment was less than full, it could always be increased and, if so desired, brought up to full by lifting the money demand schedule sufficiently. But, just as the state of the money demand schedule is liable to be affected by the level of money wage rates, so also the level of this is liable to be affected by the state of the money demand schedule; and we are faced with a problem analogous to that studied in Chapter III.

Thus, if in one of two situations the money demand schedule for labour is higher, and, as a consequence, the volume of unemployment is less, than in the other, the restraint which the fact of unemployment imposes upon wage demands is *pro tanto* weaker and, consequently, these demands are more insistent. An approximation towards full employment thus acts through wage-earners' psychology as a cause of higher wages. Hence the tendency towards larger employment will be subject to a drag. This does not imply that employment will not be larger; but it will not be so much larger as it would have been otherwise. Every step forward towards full employment, which is made when demand becomes higher, is presently followed by, say, half a step, or possibly a whole step, backwards; and there is no reason for the process to stop, no matter how high the money demand schedule for labour is raised.

Unless, therefore, money wage rates are prevented, say by legal enactment, from reacting to enhancements of money demand in the way we have been describing, in order to *maintain* full employment it is necessary that the money demand schedule for labour shall not merely be high, but shall be continually rising, spiralling upwards for ever, so that it keeps ahead of the pursuing wage rate. This entails progressive monetary inflation and so, unless productive technique is improving at corresponding speed, continuously rising prices. War-time experience, for what it is worth, supports this conclusion. It has not proved practicable to prevent wage rates from chasing the demand schedule upwards. In times of peace, with the pressure of patriotism and propaganda lacking, to do this would be far more difficult.

Thus the policy of reducing money wage rates and that of expanding money demand do not stand on exactly the same footing. As we have seen, exceptional conditions are possible in which reductions in wage rates would not benefit employment at all ; but, unless these conditions prevail — abstraction being made of friction, labour immobility, and so on — a sufficiently low level of money wage rates would ensure full employment once for all without any need for further manipulation. Sufficiently large expansions of demand, on the other hand, could always secure full employment even if the exceptional conditions referred to above did exist. In this case, however, a single once-for-all expansion would not serve — only a continuing process of successive expansions.

CHAPTER IX

FLUCTUATIONS IN THE AGGREGATE DEMAND FOR LABOUR AND UNEMPLOYMENT

In the preceding chapters we saw reason to believe that, even though the economic system were completely stable, full employment would not be established and maintained because, instead of thorough-going competition being at work among wage-earners, strong forces are in play — at all events in such a country as England — tending to keep money wage rates above the level at which employers would find it profitable to engage all would-be wage-earners. In the actual world, of course, the economic system is not stable, but is subjected to all manner of disturbances. Once more concentrating attention upon a system where wage rates are the same everywhere and labour is perfectly mobile among centres of production, let us enquire what bearing disturbances in the aggregate demand schedule for labour have upon the volume of unemployment. A full study would have to cover disturbances initiated by movements in wage rates. Here, however, these will not be discussed; only disturbances initiated on the side of money demand; though, of course, where these are associated with induced reactions on wage rates account will have to be taken of that fact.

The disturbances to be considered may be thought of as made up partly of more or less rhythmical fluctuations about a given mean position and partly of shifts in the mean position itself. Under the latter heading there is nothing to be said beyond what has been said or implied already. Therefore attention will be confined to fluctuations. Given the mean position of the demand schedule along with the number of would-be wage-earners, we have to ask in what circumstances and how far the fact of this schedule fluctuating causes unemployment. To obviate unnecessary complications — the principle is not affected — I shall suppose the fluctuations to be of a very simple kind, straightforward up-and-down movements repeated at given time intervals through a given range respectively above and below the mean.

Before our question can be usefully studied it needs to be interpreted. The most obvious interpretation is : in what circumstances and how far does the fact of fluctuation cause aggregate unemployment over good and bad times together to be larger than it would have been if the demand schedule had stood constant at a mean level intermediate between the level at which it actually does stand at different times,[1] rates of wages being taken as given? This, however, will not quite serve. For it may be that fluctuations in demand (1) evoke associated fluctuations in wage rates or (2) cause the mean rate of wages to be higher or lower than it would have been with no fluctuations ; and the effects on unemployment of these wage reactions are clearly consequences of the fact of demand fluctuations. In view of this it is appropriate to divide the discussion into three parts. In the first, reactions upon wage rates are ignored altogether ; in the second, induced *fluctuations in wage rates* are brought into account ; in the third, the effects, if any, of fluctuations in demand on the *average level of wages* are brought into account.

I

If the wage rate, supposed the same whether demand is fluctuating or fixed at a mean central level, is taken as given, we need not concern ourselves with any parts of the demand schedule in its various positions other than the

---

[1] *I.e.* so that in respect of each wage rate the quantity demanded is the average of what is demanded at that rate with higher and lower demand schedules.

points associated with that wage rate. Thus we know that the quantity of labour demanded at that wage rate with demand at its central level is A, and at each of the two other levels $(A+a)$ and $(A-a)$ respectively. We wish to know how much unemployment over the average of good and bad times together the fact of fluctuation of any given range causes, that is, how much more unemployment over the average of good and bad times together there will be if demand fluctuates about a mean through a given distance on either side of it than if it stands stable at the mean itself.

It will be well to begin by clearing out of the way what might prove a source of confusion. If employment fluctuates over a range of 5 per cent about its mean, it is an arithmetical necessity that, since employment cannot exceed 100 per cent at any time, average employment cannot exceed 95 per cent, and, therefore, average unemployment cannot fall short of 5 per cent. Thus large fluctuations of employment imply large average unemployment. Since, therefore, large fluctuations of employment can only be caused (apart from wage changes) by large fluctuations in demand, we may be tempted to infer that large fluctuations of demand cause large average unemployment, in such wise that, if the range of demand fluctuations were reduced, average unemployment would necessarily be made smaller. There are, however, two errors in this argument. First, while it is true that, with employment fluctuating over a range of 5 per cent on either side of the mean, average unemployment cannot be less than 5 per cent, and, with it fluctuating over a range of 10 per cent, average unemployment cannot be less than 10 per cent, it does not follow that average unemployment in the latter case *must* be larger than in the former. For it may be that, with a hundred men attached to an occupation, in the latter case employment varies from 80 to 100, giving average unemployment of

FLUCTUATIONS AND UNEMPLOYMENT

10 per cent, while in the former it varies from 50 to 60, giving average unemployment of 45 per cent. Of course, wider employment fluctuations *may* go with larger average unemployment, but there is no arithmetical necessity for it to do so. Secondly, while it is true that large fluctuations of employment *can only* be caused by large fluctuations of demand, it does not follow that large fluctuations of demand *must* cause large fluctuations of employment. It may be that there is full employment both when demand is high and also when it is low, the variations in demand realising themselves in variations in the number, not of men employed, but of unfilled vacancies. Thus the inference we have been considering is completely destroyed.

To get at the truth of the matter we must take a different way. It is easy to see that, if the rate of wage is such that at the central level of demand the market is exactly cleared, so that there is neither unemployment nor unfilled vacancies, the fact of fluctuation necessarily causes unemployment; and causes more of it the wider is the range of fluctuation — up to the point at which this is so wide that in bad times the demand becomes nothing. So as to cover, not only this case but also the cases in which at the central level of demand the market is not exactly cleared, we may proceed as follows.

Let N be the number of persons seeking work, A the number demanded when the demand is at the central level, and a the range of deviation of demand on either side of this.

First, consider the case in which N>A, *i.e.* there is some unemployment in central times. Then, if there were no fluctuations, unemployment would always be equal to (N - A). When there are fluctuations of range a on either side of the mean, unemployment in bad times = (N - A + a), in good times (N - A - a) or *nil*, whichever is the larger. Therefore, if a<(N - A), *i.e.* if there is some unemployment in good times, the average of unemployment over good and bad times $= \dfrac{(N-A+a)+(N-A-a)}{2} = (N-A)$.

That is to say, unemployment is the same with fluctuating as with stable demand; the fact of fluctuation causes no unemployment. If $a > (N-A)$, *i.e.* if there is no unemployment in good times, the average of unemployment over good and bad times $= \dfrac{N-A+a}{2}$. Therefore, the fact of fluctuation causes unemployment over the average of good and bad times equal to

$$\left\{\dfrac{N-A+a}{2} - (N-A)\right\} = \dfrac{a-(N-A)}{2}.$$

This is obviously larger the larger is a, up to the point at which $a = A$, where unemployment in bad times reaches its maximum possible amount, namely N. Further, $(A + a - N)$ measures the number of unfilled vacancies in good times. Therefore unemployment over the average of good and bad times is equal to one-half the unfilled vacancies in good times.

Secondly, consider the case in which $N < A$, *i.e.* there are some unfilled vacancies in central times. Then, if there were no fluctuations, there would never be any unemployment. With fluctuations there will be no unemployment in good times; in bad times unemployment equal to $\{a - (A - N)\}$ or *nil*, whichever is the greater. Hence, if $a < (A - N)$, the fact of fluctuation causes no unemployment. If $a > (A - N)$, it causes some unemployment, namely $\dfrac{a - (A - N)}{2}$, over the average of good and bad times, and causes more of it up to the point at which $a = A$; at which point unemployment in bad times is equal to N and cannot be made larger. Further, since $\{a + (A - N)\}$ measures the number of unfilled vacancies in good times, the unemployment caused over the average of good and bad times is less than half of that.

FLUCTUATIONS AND UNEMPLOYMENT

The most important, as perhaps also the most obvious, implication of this analysis is that, in the conditions here supposed, if fluctuations in the demand for labour about a given mean demand schedule leaved some labour unemployed in good times, average unemployment over good and bad times together will be the same as it would have been had the demand schedule stood stable *at* the mean. It is necessary, however, to remember that, throughout this chapter, our analysis is built on the assumption that labour is perfectly mobile. If this is forgotten, the inference may be drawn that in actual life, since there is always some unemployment even in the best of times, fluctuations of demand about a given mean, while affecting the distribution of unemployment in time, cannot affect its aggregate amount. This is not so. For, with labour imperfectly mobile, the fact that there is always some unemployment does not preclude, as it would do if labour were perfectly mobile, there being also unfilled vacancies in some centres; and, in so far as, when demand fluctuates, such unfilled vacancies are created in good times, the fact of fluctuation does affect the aggregate amount of unemployment. It makes it larger than it would otherwise have been.

II

In the preceding section the rate of wage was taken as given. A new complication has now to be introduced. In this section we take the number of men seeking work, the mean state of the demand schedule and the extent to which this fluctuates as given, and enquire how the effect on unemployment of the fact of fluctuation differs for different rates of wages.

It is easy to see that in the supposed conditions there is a level of wages at and below which in bad times there is full employment. Full employment would also obviously exist with this wage rate if the demand schedule were stable in its central position Thus this wage rate constitutes a lower limit below which the fact of fluctuation causes no unemployment. Further, given the range of fluctuations about a given mean, there is an upper limit of wage rates above which aggregate employment over good and bad times together is the same with the demand schedule fluctuating as it would be if that schedule stood stable in its mean position. Above this limit the whole of the excess demand in good times over central times translates itself into excess employment — none of it appearing as unfilled vacancies — just as the whole of the deficiency of demand in bad times translates itself into a deficiency of employment; and the excess and deficiency cancel one another. That is to say, with wage rates above this limit, the fact of fluctuation causes no unemployment.[1]

With wage rates lying between these limits in respect of fluctuations of a given range it is easy to see that the fact of fluctuation does cause unemployment in the above sense. The extent to which it does this over good and bad times together becomes larger as the wage rate rises from the minimum rate to the rate in respect of which the market would be exactly cleared (*i.e.* there would be neither unemployed men nor unfilled vacancies) if the demand schedule stood stable in the central position. This is obvious, because, until the wage rate reaches this level, every increase in it entails more unemployment with the demand schedule in the lower position, while there is no unemployment at all with the demand schedule either in the central position or in the upper position. After the wage rate has passed this level, with every further increase the excess of unemployment with fluctuating demand

[1] The lower of the two limits is necessarily lower, and the higher higher, the wider is the range through which the demand schedule fluctuates about the mean; though it is only in special circumstances that an increase in this range moves the lower of the limits downwards and the upper upwards by equal amounts. The special circumstances are that the relevant demand curves are straight lines parallel to one another.

over what it would be with stable intermediate demand becomes less, until, when the upper of the two limits described above is reached, it disappears. This is not perhaps entirely obvious. But it can easily be proved. For over any two periods together, one good and one bad, in fluctuating conditions aggregate unemployment is equal to nothing plus the number of would-be wage-earners less the demand in bad times. In stable conditions it is equal to twice the number of would-be wage-earners minus the mean demand; which is equivalent to the number of would-be wage-earners less the demand in bad times minus the demand in good times less the number of would-be wage-earners. Hence the excess of unemployment in fluctuating, as against stable conditions, over the two periods together is equal to the demand in good times less the number of would-be wage-earners. But the number of would-be wage-earners is, of course, a constant; and the demand in good times is obviously smaller, the higher is the rate of wage. Hence over the range under consideration the excess of unemployment under fluctuating as against stable conditions diminishes as the wage rate increases; which was what had to be proved.

This last result, *i.e.* that, with wage rates intermediate between the rate that clears the market at the higher level of demand and that which clears it at the central level, the fact of fluctuation causes less unemployment the higher is the rate of wages, may seem at first sight paradoxical. For, surely, the higher the wage rate is within the limits specified, the larger, other things being equal, aggregate unemployment must be. This is, of course, true. But it is not incompatible with the proposition proved above that, the higher the wage rate is, the smaller will be, not the total amount of unemployment, but the amount of it that the fact of fluctuation causes.

III

Let us now bring into account the fact that the wage rate is often in some measure responsive to variations in the demand schedule for labour, so that when, in a fluctuation, unemployment rises above the percentage proper to the central level of demand, the wage rate rises; and in the converse case falls. This responsiveness — for the moment we ignore time-lags — entails an effect on unemployment of the same kind as would be produced if the amplitude of the fluctuations in demand were diminished. Complete responsiveness might be defined as that degree of responsiveness that would neutralise these fluctuations altogether, so that their effect on unemployment was nil. In actual life, however, responsiveness is not at all likely to be complete. In periods of expansion employers might be willing to agree to substantial advances in wage rates if they were confident that, when prosperity ended, they would be able to cancel them. They know, however, that in fact this will not be easy, that elaborate processes will have to be gone through, and that their work-people will put up a strong rear-guard action. Consequently, they are chary of conceding advances, and restrict them within as narrow limits as they can. In periods of depression wage-earners, for precisely similar reasons, hold out against wage reductions, which they might be ready to concede if it were not for the difficulty that they foresee in getting them cancelled when times improve. Moreover, the fact that what is going to happen to an industry even a few months ahead can rarely be forecast with confidence makes both sides unwilling to give away more than they can help. A widespread desire for "safety first" helps to make wage rates sticky. Their responsiveness is thus sure to be incomplete, but, none the less, there is some responsiveness. In the absence of time-lags the damage which the fact of fluctuation does to aggregate unemployment can never be increased by this circumstance, and where, apart from responsiveness, some unemployment would have been caused, is diminished by it.

In actual life, however, time-lags are often substantial. The reasons for this are well known. With wage rates settled by the elaborate machinery of collective bargaining or trade boards, claims to wage increases by work-people or to decreases by employers must inevitably be based, not on what is happening at the moment, but on records of what has happened recently — records extending at the least over several months. This must be so even under purely automatic sliding scales. Where settlements are made, not automatically, but after discussion, the actual processes of discussion and negotiation absorb further time. Thus, even if there were no propensity to resist change in the minds of any of the negotiators, some appreciable lag would result from what we may call, if we like, purely mechanical causes. A good example is afforded by what happened after the 1914–18 war. In the post-war slump of 1922 money wage rates continued to rise under the impulse of the preceding post-war boom for some six months after unemployment had begun to increase.

The consequence for unemployment of these time-lags depends on the relation between the length of lag and the frequency with which upward and downward movements in the demand for labour occur. If the relation is such that responses in wage rates to shifts of demand in one direction are fully accomplished before shifts in the opposite direction set in, a lag affects only the timing, and not the amount of the reaction on unemployment. But, if the relation between length of lag and frequency of fluctuation is such that part of the response to excesses or deficiences in demand occur after these have been reversed, the issue is more complicated. The part of the response that is accomplished before reversal operates in the same sense as the whole of it would do if the whole were so accomplished. But the part that is accomplished afterwards does not. The overlapping part acts on aggregate unemployment — when it acts on it at all — in the opposite sense to the part that does not overlap, thus never lessening, and in many cases augmenting it. If the period of non-overlap and the period of overlap are equal, we may regard them as cancelling one another, so that the net effect of fluctuations on unemployment is the same as if wage rates had not been responsive at all. If the period of non-overlap is the larger, employment is more likely to be benefited than damaged by wage responsiveness; in the converse case, it is more likely to be damaged. It may even happen that fluctuations, which would be too small to cause unemployment if there were no response, may cause some when conjoined with responses that overlap.

IV

It was shown in the first section of this chapter that, if wage rates are not responsive to demand fluctuations, the fact of fluctuation cannot cause any unemployment unless conditions are such that there are unfilled vacancies in good times, and that, when this condition is satisfied, the maximum amount of unemployment over the average of good and bad times that it can cause is one-half of the number of these unfilled vacancies. If wage rates do respond to demand fluctuations, it is easy to see that the same propositions hold good of the fact of demand fluctuations plus the fluctuations in wage rates that they induce.

V

Up to this point we have supposed that the wage rate established, if wages are not responsive to demand fluctuations, is the same throughout whether demand is fixed or fluctuating; and, if wage rates are responsive, that the rate proper to a centrally situated demand schedule is the same in a fluctuating as in a stable system. There is, however, reason to think that these assumptions are often inappropriate. First, suppose that the wage rate is held constant in the face of demand fluctuations. In a fluctuating system, when demand is high, wage-earners will be more strongly placed to press for high wage rates that in a stable system ; and, though, when demand is low, they will be less strongly placed, it may well be that on balance they are more strongly placed ; so that, if the wage rate is held constant, it will be so held at a higher level in a fluctuating than in a stable system. Secondly, suppose that the wage-rate is not held constant. Then, when demand swings, it may well happen that the responding swings in wage rates will not, as we have hitherto tacitly assumed, be symmetrical for upward and downward movements. Humanitarian sentiment and State provision for unemployment set a limit below which it is impossible for wage rates to be pushed down. Thus, when fluctuations are very large, wage rates respond less to down-swings than to up-swings. The lack of response to the lower part of the down-swing entails that the mean level of wage rates is raised above what it would have been if demand had not fluctuated. Whether or not, therefore, wage rates are held constant in the face of demand fluctuations, the mean level of wage rates is likely to be higher in a fluctuating system than in a stable system in which the central level of the demand schedule is the same. On account of this indirect reaction the fact of fluctuation may be expected to cause unemployment (*i.e.* to make it larger than it would have been without the fluctuation) to a greater extent, and over a wider range of circumstance, than the preceding analysis taken by itself would suggest.

CHAPTER X

THE DISTRIBUTION OF FLUCTUATIONS OF DEMAND FOR LABOUR AMONG DIFFERENT CENTRES

In the last chapter we supposed labour to move with perfect freedom among the several centres of production and concentrated attention upon the consequences of fluctuations in the aggregate demand for labour upon employment. From the point of view of a short period the number of wage-earners attached to and seeking work at particular centres, or, at all events, at the groups of centres that constitute occupations, are often approximately fixed, so that fluctuations in particular demands, and not merely in aggregate demands, are relevant. In respect, therefore, of a given set of wage rates we now postulate a number of occupations, to each of which there is attached a definite demand schedule for labour varying over a definite range on either side of the mean, and an aggregate quantity of labour seeking work in all occupations together. We suppose that, as generally happens in fact with cyclical fluctuations, the demands for labour in different occupations move upwards or downwards in sympathy; ignoring the fact that on some occasions one demand expands while another contracts. We have then, with a given set of wage rates, a given percentage range about the mean over which aggregate demand fluctuates. How is aggregate employment likely to be affected in different circumstances if, on the one hand, the demands in all occupations fluctuate over percentage ranges that are approximately equal to this or, on the other hand, some demands fluctuate over a substantially wider, others over a narrower range?

DISTRIBUTION OF FLUCTUATIONS

If the numbers of wage-earners attached to the several occupations were determined by historical accident without regard to the conditions currently ruling there, adequate data for answering this question would be lacking. As we saw, however, in Chapter VII, forces are always at work tending, in a very rough and imperfect way no doubt, but still tending to allocate would-be wage-earners among centres in accordance with the rule of equal actuarial attractiveness. Let us suppose that in fact labour is allocated in accordance with this rule. On that supposition our question becomes reasonably clear-cut.

Let us imagine a situation in which wage rates are the same everywhere, and the percentage range of fluctuation on either side of the mean demand is 5 per cent everywhere; and let us ask what will happen to unemployment if the range of fluctuation in some centres is increased to 15 per cent while the aggregate range remains 5 per cent. It is evident that in the initial situation the average percentage of unemployment over good and bad times together must be the same everywhere; otherwise the rule of equal actuarial attractiveness is not satisfied. But this percentage need not be equal to the percentage range of fluctuation. Granted that, in the initial situation, at the lower end of the 5 per cent fluctuations there is more unemployment everywhere, three cases have to be distinguished; according as, at the upper end (i) the market is exactly cleared everywhere, so that there is neither unemployment nor unfilled vacancies anywhere, (ii) there is some unemployment everywhere, and (iii) there are some unfilled vacancies everywhere.

When the range of fluctuation in some centre is raised from 5 to 15 per cent, which implies that the range in other centres is reduced in some degree below 5 per cent, it must happen in case (i) that unemployment in the centre primarily affected is increased in the first instance in bad times, while remaining as before in good times

This entails that the actuarial attractiveness in that centre is diminished, while that of the other centres, where the range of fluctuation is contracted, remains unchanged; with the result that the number of persons attached to the centre primarily affected is cut down in such measure that the average percentage of unemployment there again becomes approximately 5 per cent. Thus initially mean demand was 100 and numbers attached 105, demand varying between 95 and 105 — a range of 5 per cent about the mean. The average unemployment percentage was $\frac{100}{105}$ times 5 per cent — approximately 5 per cent. After the change the mean demand is still 100, but the demand now varies between 85 and 115. In order that average unemployment over good and bad times together may still stand at approximately 5 per cent, the number of persons attached to the centre must be reduced from 105 to 95, with employment varying from 85 to 95. The ten men withdrawn from the affected centre can find no employment elsewhere since there are no unfilled vacancies available. But before they were withdrawn all of them were employed in good times. Therefore, even though, as in this case, none of the men were initially employed in bad times, it is plain that average employment must be reduced by the change.

In case (ii) a like result follows *provided that* the increase in the range of fluctuation in the centre primarily affected is sufficient to destroy all unemployment and create unfilled vacancies there in good times. For then the creation of these unfilled vacancies entails a reduction in the average percentage of employment and so in actuarial attractiveness, which necessitates a shift of would-be wage-earners away from the centre. But, if the increase in the range of fluctuation is not sufficient to do this and there is still some unemployment in the centre in good times, average employment and so actuarial attractiveness there is not affected, and nothing happens. Thus an adverse effect

DISTRIBUTION OF FLUCTUATIONS

is produced on employment, not by *any* increase above the average in the range of fluctuations in particular centres, but only by sufficiently large increases.

In case (iii) any increase in the range of fluctuation in a particular centre obviously adds to the number of unfilled vacancies there in good times, so decreases the actuarial attractiveness of the centre, and so drives some men out of it. But now, since in good times there are unfilled vacancies in other centres, the displaced men will find themselves as fully employed as before, so that no damage is done to aggregate employment — unless, indeed, the number of men displaced exceeds the number needed to do away altogether with unfilled vacancies elsewhere.

In view of what was said in earlier chapters there can be little doubt that of these three cases the second conforms best to actual conditions. Hence for practical purposes we may conclude that in a situation where wage rates initially are the same everywhere, while fairly small inequalities in the percentage range of demand fluctuations in different centres may well leave aggregate unemployment the same as it would have been had all the percentage ranges been equal, the existence of substantial differences among the percentage ranges is likely to make aggregate unemployment over good and bad times together larger than it would have been had all the percentages been equal.

So far we have supposed that wage rates are the same everywhere. When this is not so, it is possible that initially unemployment in good times may exist in low-wage centres and unfilled vacancies in high-wage centres; and this makes generalisation difficult. Still in a broad way we may fairly conclude that here too, while small deviations from equality in the percentage ranges of fluctuations in different centres may well make no difference to aggregate employment, large deviations will probably be unfavourable to it. Thus it is not a matter of indifference that in this country, where short-period mobility from trade to trade is very imperfect, the demand for labour fluctuates in a much larger proportion in some industries than it does in others.

The foregoing argument assumes, of course, that the wage set-up is not affected by the way in which fluctuations of demand are distributed. This is not always in fact so. Such alterations of set-up as result from substituting unequal for equal percentage fluctuations among the centres is, indeed, so it would seem, equally likely to be favourable or unfavourable to aggregate employment. But the existence of this factor of unknown tendency renders our conclusions less secure than they would otherwise have been.

CHAPTER XI

MOVEMENTS OF LABOUR IN RELATION TO UNEMPLOYMENT

In the last chapter no reference was made to current movements of labour between occupations. Labour was supposed to be standing distributed in a given way either as the result of historical accident or in consequence of its *having moved* in the past to conform with the rule of equal actuarial attractiveness. That is to say, while long-run movements of labour in response to differences in average future prospects were allowed, short-run movements in response to present differences were ruled out. Thus the question whether or how such movements, if they occurred, would affect employment did not arise. Now that question calls for study.

I

There are two conditions in which the movement of men out of centres where they are standing unemployed into other centres — nothing, of course, is gained by the movement of men already employed — make the sum-total of unemployment smaller than it would be otherwise. The first is that in the centres into which they are moved unfilled vacancies, *i.e.* posts which employers would like to fill at the ruling rate of wage if they could find tenants for them, are standing open to receive them. The second is that, while there are no unfilled vacancies standing open initially, the movement of labour reacts on wages in such a way as to induce employers in the centres to which men are moved to increase the number of their employees by more than employers in the centres from which men are moved are induced to decrease the number of theirs.

Prima facie, indeed, it might be thought that the second way is ruled out. For the movements of men out of centres where they are standing unemployed will not react on wage rates in such a way as to increase employment in the centres to which they move more than they diminish it in those from which they move; because, when men shift from centre A to centre B, the downward pressure which is exerted on wage rates in B is counterbalanced by an equivalent release from pressure at A. Hence, it seems, the effects produced on the two centres should, in general, cancel out. But this conclusion is over-facile. The reason is that in actual life, while there is no definite arrest point against upward movements of wage rates, downward movements cannot carry them below a substantial minimum. This barrier is made impassable partly by public sentiment and partly by the fact that men will not accept rates of wages below what the State is prepared to pay them if they are unemployed. Suppose, then, that demand is very low in some industries, with the result that in these industries many more men are assembled than would be sufficient to force the wage rate down to the minimum. In these conditions a large number of them may be withdrawn from those industries without wage rates there rising appreciably and, therefore, without employment there being appreciably contracted through this type of reaction. But there is no corresponding hindrance to wage rates in the industries, *to* which the men move, being forced down from their comparatively high level, and to employment in them being by this means substantially expanded; with the net result that aggregate employment is increased. Potential unfilled vacancies, that wait the entry of new men and the reductions of money wage rates to which this leads, must, therefore, be reckoned as at least of equal account with actual unfilled vacancies.

Some readers may even be tempted to argue that

movements of labour, since they do not increase money income or outlay, can only increase employment if they do lead to reductions in money wage rates. But this is a misconception. If there are a hundred men engaged in producing some commodity, and employers would like, at current wages and current prices, to engage more men, *i.e.* if there are unfilled vacancies, the filling of these vacancies at the current wage rate would necessarily entail an increase in the proportion of total income accruing to wage-earners as against non-wage-earners. Thus employment *can* be increased without either wage rates being lowered or money income being increased.

The employment-producing tendency of movements of labour towards either actual or potential unfilled vacancies is, however, in part offset. As was observed in Chapter III, when employment and, consequently, real income is increased, people tend to save more; the rate of interest, therefore, tends downwards and, again consequently, with normal monetary arrangements, aggregate money income is reduced, and so the money demand schedule for output as a whole is lowered This entails that the benefit conferred on employment from employment-producing movements is *pro tanto* reduced. For example, when the movement is out of unemployment into unfilled vacancies, it is not as large as the number of these vacancies that are seen to be filled; for some unseen unemployment is brought about indirectly at the same time. But these considerations merely qualify, they have no tendency to overthrow, the broad conclusion set out above.

II

We now suppose ourselves to start with a situation in which, while there is some unemployment everywhere, no movement of labour could increase employment, and enquire what sort of disturbance in the state of labour demands would create occasions for movements of an employment-producing kind. It is evident that a rise in the demand for labour in any centre will not do this unless it is large enough to prevent any unemployed men from being left standing in that centre — and this quite irrespective of anything that may be happening to the demand for labour elsewhere. It *can* do it only if the rise is such that, unless men move in from elsewhere, unfilled vacancies will exist in the centre where it has occurred. If that condition is satisfied, it *will* do it, provided that, apart from movement, some men would be standing unemployed in other centres. This proviso *must* be satisfied if the rise in demand in our centre has been compensatory to a net downward movement in other centres. Moreover, apart from an abnormal all-embracing boom, it is likely to be satisfied even though the rise has been complementary to a net rise elsewhere. It would be a great mistake to suppose that no opportunity for employment-producing movements of labour could be created by an expansion of demand in centre A unless there were a contemporary contraction or, at all events, no contemporary expansion in centre B. Plainly, however, the extent of the opportunity for employment-producing movements is likely, other things being equal, to be larger if demands in other centres are falling than if they are rising; for a fall in these demands increases, while a rise diminishes the number of men for whom movement out of unemployment into employment is possible. Thus the chance of substantial opportunities for employment-producing movements of labour manifesting themselves are more favourable where the movements in the demands for labour in different centres are compensatory than where they are complementary. It is, therefore, relevant to our problem to distinguish certain principal types of movement from this point of view.

Consider first those general movements lasting several years that are usually called cyclical. There is now substantial agreement among economists that the motive force immediately behind these movements, so far as they are autonomous and not induced by variations in foreign demand for exports, consists in variations in the desire of entrepreneurs (including the Government) to engage substantially more or less labour than usual in some field of work not closely geared to the production of those ordinary consumption goods to which the public are already accustomed. These up-swings and down-swings of desire for new construction are reflected in corresponding swings in entrepreneurs' desires for money with which to finance employment in erecting the structures that constitute real investment. *Prima facie* this might be provided equally well either through money income being diverted from labour and equipment engaged in making consumption goods or through new money income being brought into being. It is not to be expected, however, that such moderate rise in the rate of interest as is generated by entrepreneurs' increased desire to make investments will cause people to contract their consumption to any significant extent in order to hand over income to these entrepreneurs. Therefore, such extra money as is devoted to investment has to come in the main through extra money income being brought into being; that is through transfers of existing money from passive to active stocks and the creation by the banks of new money to put into these latter stocks. Thus at the first stage investment will be increased while expenditure on, and amount of, consumption is somewhat diminished, or, at all events, is not increased. But this arrangement is not what the public want or is prepared to maintain. When their real income is enlarged they are only, in general, willing to take out more in investment provided they can take out more in consumption also. They may, indeed, be *forced* to depart from this rule temporarily through the in-swing of new money income, but the resultant situation is not a stable one. At the second stage, therefore, *e.g.* in the second income period, in order to maintain the high rate of investment that has been set up, the process of augmenting active money, and so money income, has to be repeated. Thus suppose that initially money income consisted of C pounds paid for consumption and V pounds paid for investment, and that, through an expansion of entrepreneurs' desire, money investment is raised in a first income period to $(V+X)$, and money income, therefore, to $(C+V+X)$. In the second period, out of the total money income $(C+V+X)$, less than $(V+X)$ will be devoted to investment, This entails that more will be devoted to buying consumption goods, with the result that the prices of consumption goods rise. This entails again that there is an extra profit to be got by employing wage-earners — at a given money wage — to make these goods. Therefore more money income is turned to hiring labour for that purpose; until a new equilibrium is established, with income distributed between investment and consumption in the proportion that the public desire. If the extra income called into being to finance the extra investment in the first income period were all available in the second period to finance that amount of extra investment over again, there would be no mechanism available to bring about increased demand for labour in industries making consumption goods. As things are, there is such a mechanism. The money demands for labour in the investment industries and in the consumption industries swing up — and in like manner, of course, swing down — together. The movements of the several parts of aggregate demand associated with cyclical fluctuations are, in the main, complementary, not compensatory.

Consider, secondly, large-scale disturbances, sometimes called structural, that are not cyclical in character, but are, rather, once-for-all changes, such as are induced by the decay of an old-established industry in consequence of the introduction of a rival product or the loss of an export market: or, on a different footing, such as occur in transitions from peace to war or from war to peace. Once-for-all changes other than those connected with these transitions are similar in general character to the cyclical changes described above.[1] Like them and through the same type of mechanism, they may be expected to generate complementary sets of demand movements. There is no need, therefore, to discuss them further. War and peace transitions are, however, different in character. It is convenient to consider separately peace-to-war and war-to-peace shifts.

When a country passes from peace to war we may say, if we will, that the people come to desire soldiers' services and war-like equipment in place of ordinary civilian goods. But there are alternative ways in which this shifting of desire may manifest itself. It may happen that the Government finances the war predominantly by creating new money. In that case the money demand schedule for labour for military purposes and that for civilian purposes both expand, the former, of course, expanding much more than the latter. The movements of different parts of the demand schedule are thus complementary. Alternatively, it may happen that the Government finances the war in large part by taxes and loans from the general public, so that the purchasing power available for civilian use is reduced while that available for military use is increased. In this case the movements of different parts of demand schedule are compensatory. In England during the present war the movements of military and civilian money demand have had this character.

When a country passes from war to peace — if the war has been on a large scale — it might conceivably happen that so violent a deflation occurred as to make the money demand schedule for civilian purposes as well as

[1] Sometimes the unemployment arising out of them is spoken of as " structural unemployment " and contrasted with the " general unemployment " that is supposed to be connected with trade cycles. This is an unfortunate use of language. Structural changes in the literal sense almost always accompany the trade cycle.

that for war purposes contract, so that the movements in the two fields are complementary. But experience suggests that, at least in the immediate aftermath of war, this is unlikely. We may be fairly sure that civilian money demand will expand while military money demand contracts, *i.e.* that the two movements will be compensatory.

There remain to be considered, thirdly, those "seasonal fluctuations", which are associated with variations in climate or climate-generated fashion. As between some sorts of labour these occasion complementary movements of demand. Firing and light, for example, are both more needed in winter than in summer. As between others they occasion compensatory movements. Less builders' work and more coal-miners' work is needed in winter. Alongside of these movements may be set those that are continually taking place inside separate industries as one firm grows and another declines. Such movements are, of course, compensatory.

III

In some conditions *what appear to be* employment-producing movements of labour tend to come about of their own accord — through the play of economic motives. This will be so when centres of relatively great actuarial attractiveness are also centres of relatively good employment; as they must be when high wages and good employment are associated together. This association is frequently found. For example, in the disturbed period following the last war low wages and large unemployment were combined in one group of industries, the unsheltered group, and high wages and better employment in the sheltered group. Again, writing in 1929, Mr. Henry Clay found: "Wage rates already are lowest by pre-war standards in the industries suffering most from unemployment and highest in the industries suffering least".[1] In conditions such as these there is obviously a strong tendency

[1] *The Post-War Unemployment Problem*, p. 155.

for movements of labour of an employment-producing kind to take place of their own accord.

IV

It must be observed, however, that *what appear to be* employment-producing movements are not always so in fact. Their efficacy in actually promoting employment is often hampered, and may even be reversed, by the fact that the movements are not accomplished instantaneously. This consideration is more important than it might seem to be at first sight. It is, for example, obvious, as a simple arithmetical calculation shows, that, if the average movement from job to job occupied three days and everybody changed his job once a year, the statistical record would show 1 per cent unemployment. Because of the time lost in the actual process of movement, the British Government during the war have deliberately *restricted* movement from firm to firm in certain important industries, with the object of preventing people from losing in movement time that might have been occupied on jobs.

Of greater moment is the fact that, especially when industries are separated by large differences in training and technique, stimuli to movement are translated into action, not at once, but gradually over a considerable period of time. In this movements of labour resemble changes in rates of wages, which, as we saw in Chapter IX, sometimes work like delayed-action, rather than like contact, bombs. Thus suppose that initially the actuarial attractiveness of centre A is the same as that of centre B; and that presently a relative rise in the demand at A makes that centre more attractive than the other. A tendency will be set up for labour to move from B to A. But of those obstacles to movement that are due to be overcome eventually not all will be overcome at once; and it may well be that a considerable period elapses before the tendency works itself out fully.

The delay is likely to be especially long when shifts in the relative demands for labour in different centres are met chiefly, not by the physical movement of persons already attached to less favoured into more favoured ones, but by new recruits, who are growing up to working age, being switched over from the former towards the latter set. In such cases the delay in reactions on movement, just like the delay referred to in Chapter IX in reactions on wage rates, may sometimes entail that what should have been a corrective to unemployment in fact aggravates it. For, as a result of the delay, when demand in a centre or set of centres first expands and presently contracts, the influx of men induced by the expansion may take place in large part after the contraction has set in. A notable example of this kind of maladjustment was the continuing large flow of new recruits into the coal-mining industry of this country during the mid-1920s in spite of the fact that the coal industry was then greatly depressed and suffering from heavy unemployment. The maladjustment here was so marked that an Act of Parliament was passed in 1926 designed to restrict for the time being the further recruiting for the industry of persons under eighteen.

Of course, it will not always happen that these time-lags in movement cause misfits damaging to employment. Sometimes the net effect of an expansion of demand in some set of centres in drawing men there will have worked itself out before any subsequent contraction takes place — if it ever does take place. Sometimes the general trends in numbers present and numbers demanded may move together appropriately, overriding, so to speak, short-period disharmonies. Still, it is reasonable to suppose that the existence of these time-lags render the movements of labour towards unfilled vacancies or potential unfilled vacancies that come about of their own accord less effective in promoting aggregate employment than it would be if they did not exist.

V

So far we have been considering conditions in which what appear to be employment-producing movements of labour tend to come about of their own accord. We saw, however, in Chapter VII that, as between centres, in some of which the demand for labour is much less elastic than in others, wage-earners may well succeed in putting rates of wages higher in the centres of lower demand-elasticity. If this happens, labour will be attracted towards those centres, maybe forming there pools of unemployment, even though there are unfilled vacancies in other centres. In these conditions the movements of labour that tend to come about of their own accord are, apart altogether from time-lags, not employment-producing, but rather employment-destroying. Whether for this reason or because some movements of an employment-producing kind, which do tend to come about of their own accord, are liable to be delayed, or even stopped, by ignorance and inertia, occasions may arise from time to time when there is a strong case for direct State action to stimulate the transfer of work-people away from occupations where unemployment has become abnormally large towards other occupations, where either unfilled vacancies already exist or where there is a fair prospect that the entry of new men may react on wage rates in such a way as to create them. Such occasions are especially likely to present themselves after large-scale once-for-all disturbances, when many men find their old skills unwanted and are unable to pass out of unemployment into actual or potential unfilled vacancies until they have received training in new ones. It would be wrong, however, to lay down a general rule that *any* movement of labour which would be employment-producing if it came about, but would not come about of its own accord, ought to be assisted by the State. Suppose it costs £1000 worth of effort to move a man from job A to job B, and he would only be wanted in job B long enough to produce £100 worth of goods. It would be much more economical for the community to keep him at A and pay him £100 for doing nothing than to undertake the cost of moving him. This is, of course, an extravagant example, but it illustrates a real point. Unemployment is always an evil, but sometimes to reduce it might entail worse evils.

CHAPTER XII

STABILISING THE DEMAND FOR LABOUR

IN current discussions of the unemployment problem a dominant part is played by proposals to stabilise aggregate demand, or, more strictly, the aggregate money demand schedule for labour. For a thorough treatment of this matter we should have to take note of the fact that, when the number of would-be wage-earners is changing, there is a choice between stabilizing demand absolutely and stabilizing it per head of would-be wage-earners; the latter arrangement being preferable on several grounds. Here, however, we need not trouble about this, but may suppose the number of would-be wage-earners to be roughly constant, so that stabilization per head and in an absolute sense come to the same thing. In these conditions there are two alternative forms of stabilisation, according as it is achieved by lowering the demand schedule proper to good times and raising that proper to bad times, so as to settle it permanently at a level intermediate between the two, or by leaving the higher demand schedule unchanged and raising the lower one to a level with it. The former sort of stabilisation is exemplified by policies directed to transfer expenditures, *e.g.* on building schools, roads, and so on, from periods of boom to periods of depression, or, indirectly, by financing Government expenditure in depressions out of bank loans, thus leaving private persons with more money to spend than they would have had if these expenditures had been financed out of taxes, and repaying the loans out of extra taxes in good times. The latter sort is represented by policies directed to increase expenditures in bad times without any corresponding cut in good times, as, for example, by a special programme of public works of a kind that it would not be socially worth while to carry out at all if, in order to do this, labour had to be withdrawn from other tasks, but which it is socially worth while to carry out if otherwise the labour would have been unemployed. Though, as we have seen, some, it may be considerable, advantage for employment would follow from the former sort of stabilisation, it is the latter sort — stabilisation upwards — on which men's hopes of solving the problem of unemployment are now chiefly pinned.

There has been a great deal of discussion about methods by which it is claimed that this kind of stabilisation could and should be brought about. The problem is a technical one, less simple than it might seem to be at first sight, but, none the less, in principle clearly capable of solution. I do not propose to go over that familiar ground or to debate the comparative advantages of operating primarily upon investment demand or consumption demand. But there are two points upon which a brief cautionary comment may not be out of place.

First, in current discussions, as it seems to me, too little account is taken of the fact that the aggregate demand for labour is made up of demands directed to many different centres, between some of which, at all events in the short run, labour does not move at all freely. In view of this fact, merely to raise the aggregate money demand for labour in bad times to what it is in good times will not necessarily suffice to raise aggregate employment to what it is then. What happens depends partly upon the way in which the impetus to enhanced demand is distributed in bad times between various centres and occupations and partly upon the degree of freedom with which labour is able, or is encouraged, to move to those centres and occupations where demand has been stimulated out of others where it has become depressed Complete success is not to be expected. A portion of the stimulated demand can hardly fail to waste itself in creating unfilled vacancies — associated with special profits for non-wage-earners. Thus the extent to which aggregate employment can be benefited by an increase in the demand for new houses is limited, not merely by the total number of men out of work, but by that part of them who are already in, or are capable of being moved into, the building industry. More generally, expansions in demand for labour through public works, concentrated on particular fields where for political reasons Government can operate easily, might prove relatively ineffective unless unemployment at the time happened to be especially large in those fields. Thus, if our aim is to help employment, it is necessary to think, not merely of the quantity, but also of the quality, or distribution, of aggregate effective demand. A solution is not to be found in stabilising upwards each separate part of the aggregate. For this would mean stagnation. " A system — any system, economic or other — that at *every* given point of time fully utilises its possibilities to the best advantage may yet in the long run be inferior to a system that does so at *no* given point of time, because the latter's failure to do so may be a condition for the level or speed of long-run performance." [1]

Looking this difficulty in the face and passing on, we observe, secondly, that what was said in Chapter VIII about a stable economy is equally applicable to the disturbed or fluctuating economy of real life. When the aggregate money demand for labour is pushed up in bad times towards the level at which it stands in good times, just as when, all times being alike, it is pushed up in all, and when, in consequence, unemployment is reduced, this very fact encourages wage-earners to press for improved money wage rates. So far as they succeed in securing these, the effect of enhanced money demand for

---

[1] Schumpeter, *Capitalism, Socialism, and Democracy*, p. 8

labour in increasing employment will be partially offset. Unless a spiralling movement of inflation is allowed to develop, so that the money demand for labour is not merely stabilised upwards, but perpetually moves higher and higher ahead of the pursuing wage rate, it may be completely or almost completely destroyed.

There is, indeed, no reason why *some* measure of inflation — continuing expansion of money income or money income per head — should *not* be allowed to develop. If technique is improving and capital equipment growing, without inflation in this sense general prices must tend downwards; and most people would agree that an inflationary movement not more than adequate to stabilise general prices is, at the worst, innocuous. An inflation of higher degree than this strikes hardly at the recipients of fixed incomes and incomes which, though not absolutely fixed, are especially difficult to raise — the incomes, for example, of University professors! But that does not mean the end of the world! No doubt, a run-away, or galloping, inflation is disastrous, the father of chaos. But a moderate inflationary tendency, if it enables unemployment to be kept at a low level, would be well worth enduring. It is doubtful, however, whether a moderate inflation would prove sufficient to ensure a really good employment situation.

Unless it proves sufficient, and *a fortiori* if inflation is ruled out altogether and reliance placed on simple stabilisation upwards, in order for unemployment to be kept at a low level, trade unions must refrain from regarding good employment as a ground for insisting on increased money rates of wages. They must *choose* between higher rates of wages and lower rates of unemployment. During the inter-war period the average percentage of unemployment in this country was between two and three times what it had been before 1914. During that same period State provision for unemployed persons was enormously improved, so that the effect of heavy unemployment in deterring trade unions from pressing for high money wage rates was much weakened. It would be unreasonable to hold that the second of these facts had no bearing upon the first. This aspect of the unemployment problem meets with scant attention in current discussion. It is not a popular theme. The more, therefore, is it the duty of an academic economist to focus attention upon it.

THE END